When I'm At Work

Doctor

Written by Deborah Chancellor
Photography by Chris Fairclough

W
FRANKLIN WATTS
LONDON•SYDNEY

First published in 2005 by Franklin Watts
96 Leonard Street, London EC2A 4XD

Franklin Watts Australia
45-51 Huntley Street, Alexandria, NSW 2015

© Franklin Watts 2005

Editors: Caryn Jenner, Sarah Ridley
Designer: Jemima Lumley
Art direction: Jonathan Hair
Photography: Chris Fairclough

The publisher wishes to thank Joe, Lorraine, Luke, Reece and
Rachel, and all the staff at the Groom Road Surgery for their
assistance with the book.

A CIP catalogue record for this book is available from the
British Library.

ISBN 0 7496 6056 2

Dewey decimal classification number: 610.69

Printed in China

Contents

I am a doctor

My name is Joe Ovuike. I am a doctor.
Doctors help sick people to get better.

I work at a doctor's surgery.
Every day, patients come
to see me at the surgery.

I arrive at work early in the morning. Yvonne the receptionist gives me some patient notes to read.

People phone the surgery if they want to see a doctor. Yvonne makes appointments on the computer.

In the surgery

My patients wait in the waiting room. I call them when it is their turn to see me.

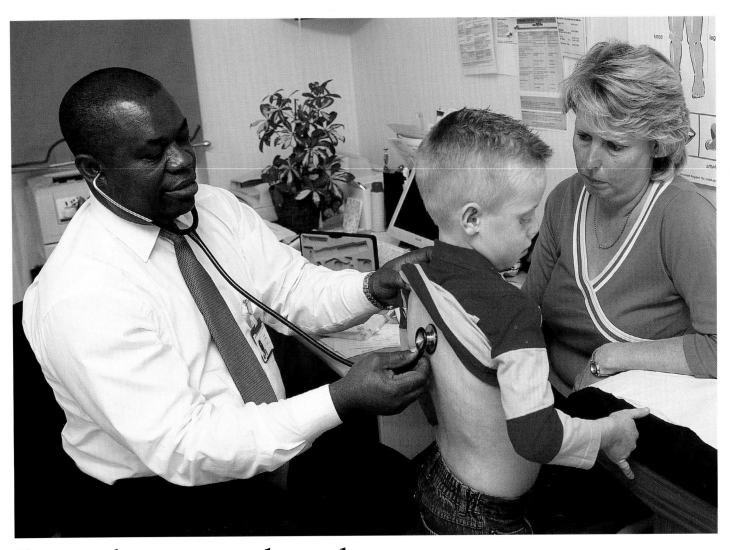

Reece has a cough and gets
breathless very easily.
First, I listen to his heart and
lungs with my stethoscope.

An asthma check-up

I ask Reece to blow into a peak flow meter. This shows me how well his lungs are working.

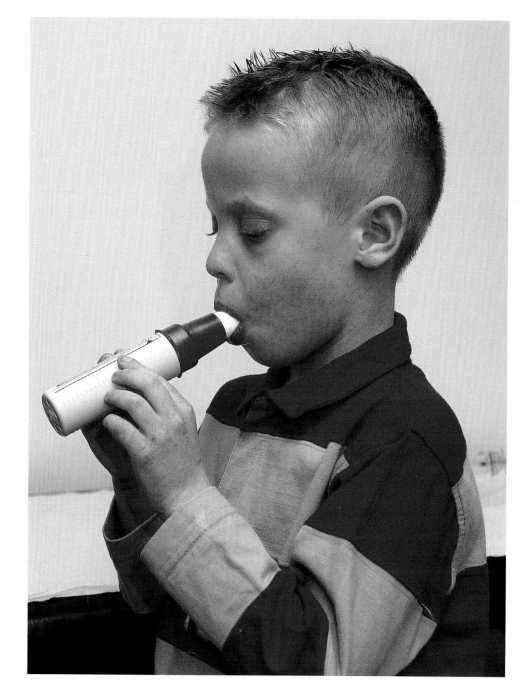

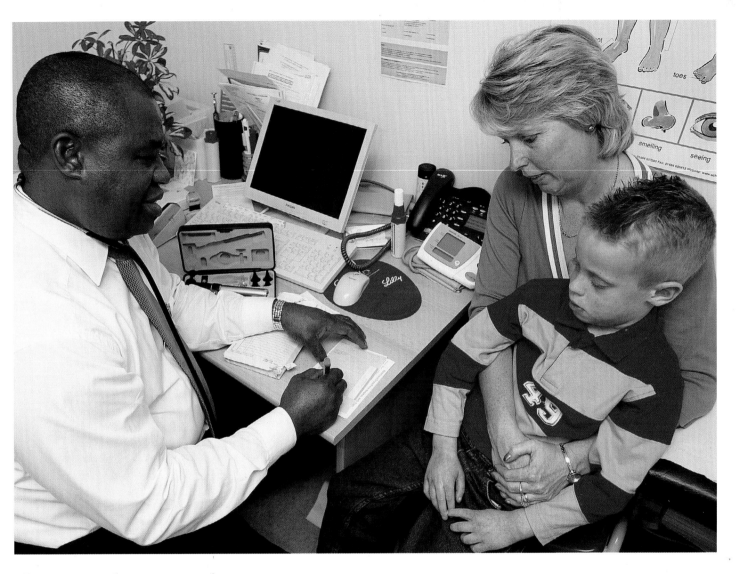

Reece has asthma.

I sign a prescription for an inhaler.

This will help him to breathe more easily.

A home visit

If my patients are too sick to come to the surgery, I visit them at home. I go on home visits after the morning appointments.

I take my doctor's bag with me when I go on home visits. I have all the equipment I need in my bag.

At a patient's house

Luke is feeling ill. I put a thermometer in his ear, to take his temperature. It is 40°C, which is very high.

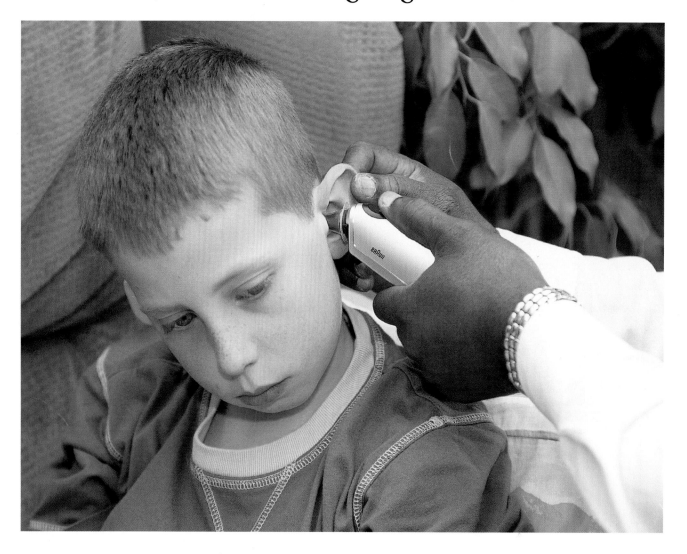

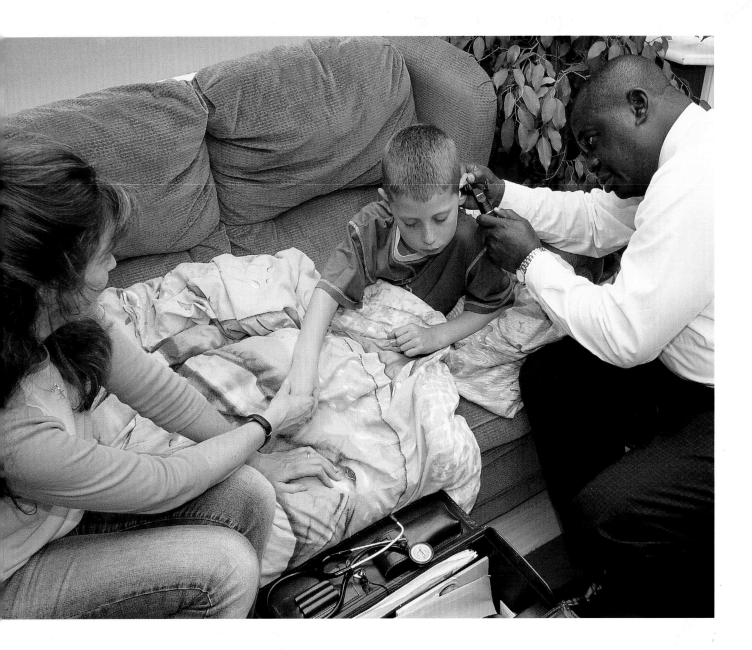

I look in Luke's ears with an
instrument called an otoscope.

Giving advice

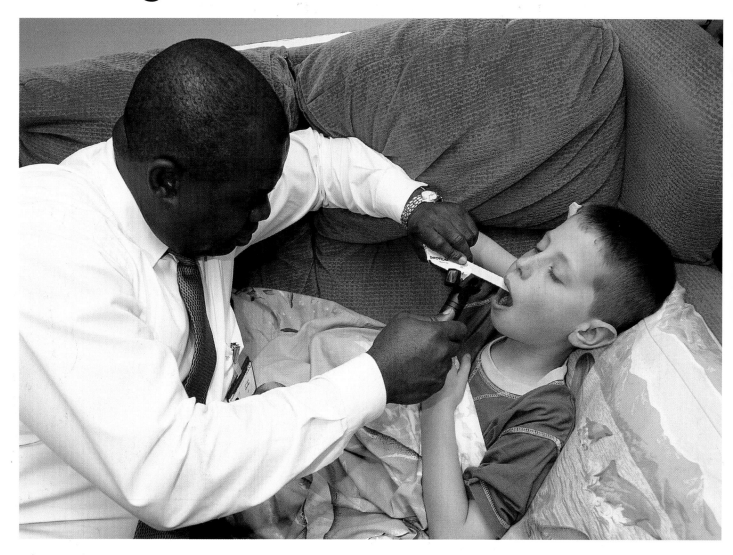

I also look in Luke's throat with my otoscope.
Luke has got 'flu. This is why his temperature
is so high.

I tell Luke's mum to give him plenty to drink, and to let him sleep a lot. His temperature will go down, and then he will feel much better.

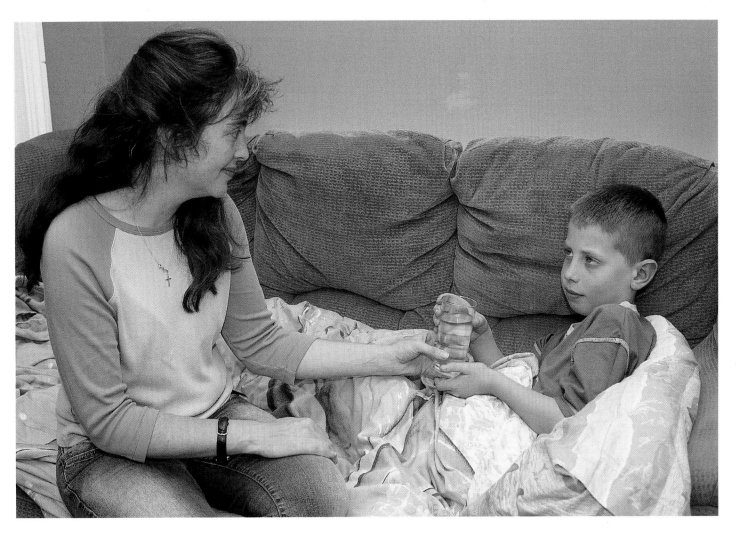

An emergency patient

Sometimes emergency patients
arrive at the surgery.
Rachel feels very dizzy, and is about to faint.

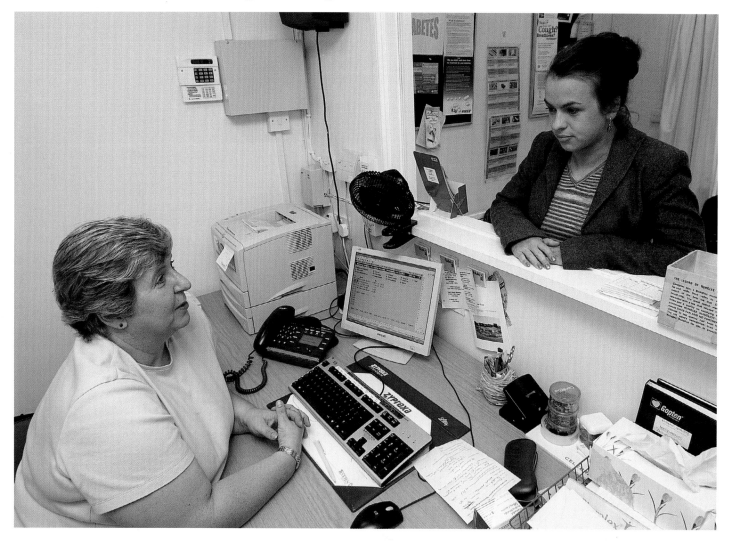

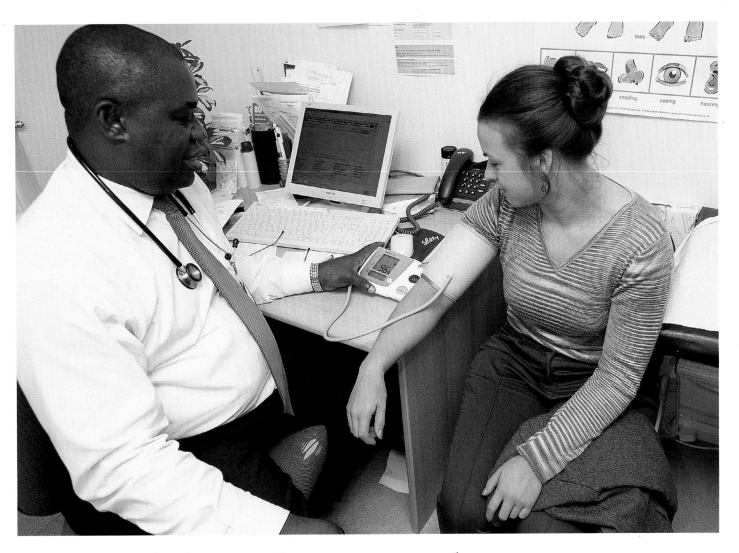

I see Rachel straight away and
measure her blood pressure.
Rachel's blood pressure is too high.
She may have a heart problem.

Off to hospital

Rachel needs to go to hospital. I phone the hospital and write a letter for Rachel to give to the hospital doctors.

Rachel's friend takes her straight to the hospital.

Meetings

The people who work at my surgery
are always very busy.
We meet together to talk about our work.

The doctors take it in turns to see patients in the evenings. When it isn't my turn, I say goodbye, and leave to go home.

A doctor's equipment

The doctor looks in your mouth and ears with an **otoscope**.

Your temperature is measured with a **thermometer**.

A **blood pressure meter** measures the level of your blood pressure.

A **peak flow meter** measures how well your lungs are working.

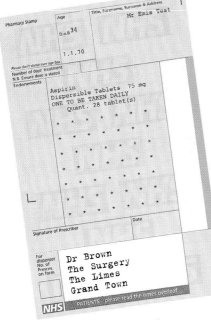

The doctor writes down the name of the medicine or equipment you need on a **prescription**.

The doctor listens to your heart and lungs with a **stethoscope**.

Looking after yourself

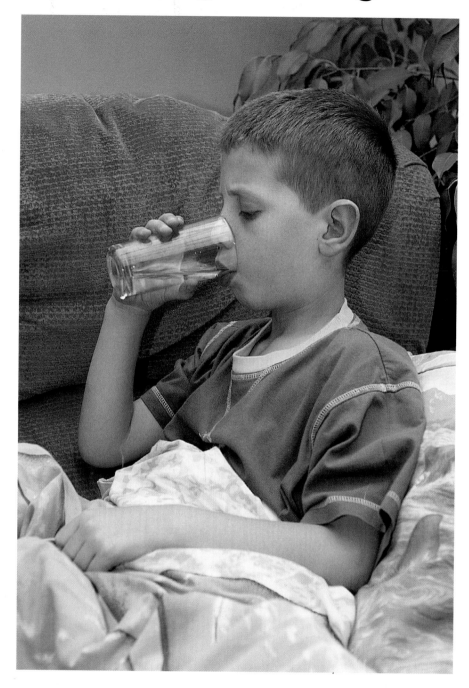

When you feel ill, you can get hot and sweaty. This is because you have a high temperature. You need to drink lots of liquid, to replace the water you have lost as sweat.

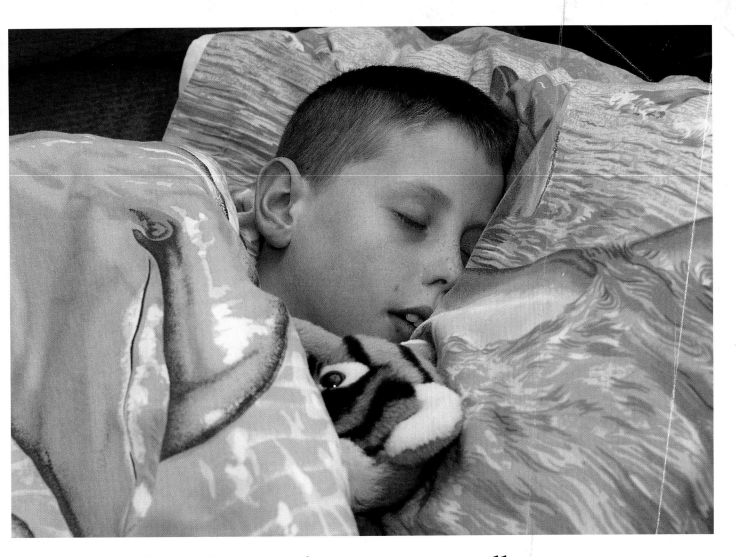

You need to sleep when you are ill.
Your body is tired and has to rest.
Sleep helps you to save energy for fighting
the germs in your body.

Glossary and index